STARS OF SPORT

MIA HAMM

BY STEPHEN CURRIE

D0204538

KIDHAVEN
PRESS™

THOMSON

™

GALE

San Diego • Detroit • New York • San Francisco • Cleveland
New Haven, Conn. • Waterville, Maine • London • Munich

THOMSON

—★—™

GALE

This book belongs t

LIBRARY OF CONGRESS CATALOGING-IN-PUBLICATION DATA

Currie, Stephen, 1960–
    Mia Hamm / by Stephen Currie.
    p. cm.—(Stars of sport)
    Summary: Discusses the childhood, soccer successes, fame, charitable works, and future options of Olympian Mia Hamm.
    Includes bibliographical references (p.   ) and index.
    ISBN 0-7377-1394-1 (alk. paper)
    1. Hamm, Mia, 1972—Juvenile literature. 2. Soccer players—United States—Biography—Juvenile literature. 3. Women soccer players— United States—Biography—Juvenile literature. [1. Hamm, Mia, 1972– 2. Soccer players. 3. Women—biography.] I. Title. II. Series.
    GV942 .7 .C87 2003
    796.354'092—dc21

    2002006975

Printed in the United States of America

Contents

CHAPTER ONE

Becoming an Athlete

Mia Hamm was born on March 17, 1972, in Selma, Alabama. But she did not live there for very long. Mia's father, William, was an officer in the U.S. Air Force, and his job took the Hamm family all over the world. Before she was six, Mia had lived in five different places: Alabama, California, Italy, Virginia, and Texas.

Mia was one of six children. Mia's name at birth was actually Mariel, but no one ever called her that. Stephanie Hamm, Mia's mother, had been a ballet dancer, and her new baby reminded her of a ballet teacher she had known. The teacher's name was Mia, so Mrs. Hamm started calling her little girl Mia. The name stuck.

Because of her own background in ballet, Mrs. Hamm was eager to have Mia learn to dance. Dancing lessons made sense, too, for another reason: Mia was a very active little girl who was always jumping and running. Mia

Mia Hamm is considered by many to be the world's greatest woman soccer player.

had her first lesson at the age of five. She hated it. The slippers pinched her feet, the class bored her, and Mia wanted to go home. She lasted only one day.

Sports

Fortunately, Mia had another interest: sports. Her father loved sports, and many of Mia's five brothers and sisters were very athletic. The oldest children played in organized sports leagues. When Mia was three or four years old she would go to their games and run around the sidelines playing with a ball of her own. When she turned five, she was thrilled to start playing on a league soccer team.

Mia and her brothers and sisters also played baseball, basketball, and football with other kids in the neighborhood. Mia's older brother Garrett, who was adopted by the family when Mia turned five, was usually one of the first to be picked in these games. Then he would insist that the team captain choose Mia. At first the captains were not pleased. After all, Mia was small and young.

But Mia was a fast runner, and she played hard. The older kids soon realized that Mia was quite an athlete. "If they snickered when Garrett picked his little sister," Mia remembered years later, "they weren't laughing at the end of the game."[1]

Choosing Soccer

Mia did well at many different sports. The more she played, the better she became. In seventh grade she was the only girl to play on her junior high school football team. She was also one of the first girls in Texas to play Little League baseball.

But soccer was Mia's favorite. Although she was too small to be a big star in basketball or football, soccer was just about a perfect match. Soccer players do not have to be big, just quick and strong, and Mia was both. "As far back as I can remember," she says, "I played [soccer] all the time at recess in grade school."[2]

Mia Hamm poses for a seventh grade yearbook photo.

Mia had a real talent for soccer, too. One year, she led her league in scoring. Often two or even three players on the other team would defend her when she had the ball. It did not matter. Mia either dribbled right past them, or she passed the ball to a teammate who was not being guarded.

And the older Mia got, the better she became. When she was fourteen Mia joined an all-girls team which traveled to games in different cities. The team included many of the best girl soccer players in all of Texas. Some of these girls were a few years older than Mia, but she liked the challenge.

The Big Time

Still, Mia did not think of herself as an outstanding soccer player. At the age of fourteen she was just pleased to make her varsity soccer team in high school. Looking past that seemed silly to her. Good as she was, she did not believe that she was anything special.

During a developmental team game, Mia Hamm (18) dribbles the ball around a defender.

That changed when she met John Cossaboon. Cossaboon was the coach in charge of the American women's **developmental team**. The developmental team was made up of the country's best high school and college players. Team members spent several weeks a year practicing and playing games. The best of them would someday play for Team USA, the national women's team.

Cossaboon saw Mia in a game, and he noticed her skills and leadership right away. When he heard that she was just fourteen, he was astonished. After the game Cossaboon invited Mia to play on the developmental team. Mia and her parents were surprised, but they quickly accepted the coach's offer.

Team USA

The developmental team did not practice year-round. The players had to go to school, so the team only got together for several weeks each year. Mia spent most of the next year at home, where she played soccer on her high school team.

But when the developmental team did meet, Mia impressed Cossaboon with her skills, her hard work, and her willingness to learn. After Mia's first year on the team Cossaboon decided it might be time for her to move up to the national team.

The national team was coached by Anson Dorrance, who also ran the women's soccer team at the University of North Carolina (UNC). Cossaboon told Dorrance about Mia. At first Dorrance thought that his friend was teasing him. Team USA was full of players who were in college, or even beyond. It was hard to imagine a fifteen-year-old joining them.

But when Dorrance saw Mia play, he changed his mind—and invited her to try out for the team. The first step was for her to come to a special training camp. The training camp was not just for players who hoped to

University of North Carolina coach and former Team USA coach, Anson Dorrance.

Mia Hamm pushes the ball forward in a Team USA game against Canada. In 1987 she became the youngest American woman to play in an international soccer match.

make the team; it was also for the women who had been team members the year before. The women at the camp were the very best female soccer players anywhere in the United States.

Mia was a hard worker. But she was not prepared for the workouts at the training camp. On the first day, the players spent several hours indoors lifting weights and stretching. The workout was exhausting. Then, just when Mia thought the day was over, the players headed to the soccer field for even more drills and practices.

But Mia did not give up. And Dorrance liked what he saw. At the end of training camp, he picked her for the team. Mia was surprised—and delighted. In August 1987 Team USA traveled to China for two games against the Chinese national team. Mia got into one of the games as a substitute, becoming the youngest American woman to play an international soccer game.

Being a part of the team was quite an achievement for Mia. But she was not content to stop there.

Titles and Championships

Although she was only a reserve on Team USA at first, Hamm knew that she was a strong offensive player. She usually played the position of **forward**. Forwards are the players most likely to shoot and score, and Hamm did both of these things quite well.

But soccer teams do not play offense the whole game. When the opponents have the ball, players have to go on defense and take the ball away from the other team. Even the forwards have to help out on defense. Hamm knew that her defensive skills were not nearly as good as her ability to score goals.

So she worked on her defense. At team practices she concentrated on taking the ball away from opponents. But Hamm worked after practice was over, too. "I'd go out to the park by myself every day and practice my skills for hours,"[3] she remembered. Little by little, she became a better player—on defense as well as on offense.

School

In the 1980s few people paid much attention to women's soccer. Men's teams played a **World Cup** tournament every four years, but there was no World Cup for women. Nor did women play soccer in the **Olympics**. Some soccer officials were trying to change that, but in the meantime Team USA only played a few games a

Hamm (9) knocks a Danish mid-fielder off the ball with a strong defensive shoulder tackle.

year. Most of the time, Hamm was at home, going to high school and playing soccer on her school's team.

After her second year of high school in Texas, though, Hamm and her family moved to northern Virginia. Hamm was willing to play soccer for her new high school—but she did not think that would be the best use of her time. Being on a high school team could not challenge her the way the national team did.

Besides, Hamm was looking ahead. Anson Dorrance, the national team coach, had already invited her to play for him at the University of North Carolina. Hamm was eager to learn from UNC's players and from Dorrance himself. After thinking it over, she arranged to take two years of high school classes in just one year. That way, she would graduate from high school early—and begin UNC early too.

Luckily, Hamm was a strong student who worked hard in class and got good grades. But the workload was tough. Between studying and soccer, there was little time left over for friends or family. But she completed the classes she needed to graduate—and led her team to the state championship. Now she was on her way to UNC.

College

UNC had by far the most successful women's soccer program among U.S. colleges. The team, called the Tarheels, had won several national championships. The roster included many of the country's best players. When Hamm joined the team in the fall of 1988, the Tarheels had not lost a game in three years.

Members of the North Carolina women's soccer team douse coach Anson Dorrance with water after their victory in 2001.

Joining the Tarheels, though, was a little scary for Hamm. Coach Dorrance planned to put her in the starting lineup, even though she was only a freshman. On Team USA she had been mostly a substitute, but here at UNC she would be a key member of the team. She worried that she would not be ready.

There was another problem, too. Hamm was not sure how the older Tarheels would respond to her. Because she was new to the team, Hamm was afraid that some of the other players would resent her. That was especially true because she was a starter, which meant that she was taking playing time away from some of the others.

Hamm knew she still had much to learn. She offered her teammates support, and she treated them with respect. In turn, the other players treated her the same way. Soon Hamm was one of the team's leaders.

Big News

Hamm enjoyed her first year at UNC very much. The Tarheels won the national college championship, and Hamm was one of the team's biggest stars. The team repeated as champions in 1990, too, and Hamm was voted the best player in all of women's soccer.

But during Hamm's second college season, soccer officials made an important announcement. They decided to hold a World Cup tournament for women, just as they already did with the men. The tournament was scheduled for China in the fall of 1991, and Team USA would be invited.

It was a great opportunity. The level of play at the tournament would be much higher than Hamm was used to in college. The teams from Norway and China, especially, were very strong. Hamm was eager to compete against the best players in the world.

Playing for the national team would mean leaving UNC for a year. Hamm was sorry to do that; still, it was an easy choice. She knew she could always come back for her final two years of college after the tournament— and she did not want to miss the first World Cup ever.

World Cup 1991

Most people did not think that Team USA had a shot at winning the tournament. But Hamm believed that her

Hamm's International Soccer Statistics

Year	Record	Games Played	Goals	Assists	Points
National Team					
1987	4-2-1	7/4	0	0	0
1988	3-3-2	8/7	0	0	0
1989	0-0-1	1/0	0	0	0
1990	5-0-0	5/1	4	1	9
1991	21-6-1	28/24	10	4	24
1992	0-2-0	2/2	1	0	2
1993	12-4-0	16/16	10	4	24
1994	8-1-0	9/9	10	5	25
1995	17-2-2	21/20	19	18	56
1996	21-1-1	23/23	9	18	36
1997	14-2-0	16/16	18	6	42
1998	18-1-2	21/21	20	20	60
1999	22-2-2	26/26	13	16	42
2000	20-5-8	33/29	13	14	40
Total	165-30-20	215/197	127	104	356
World Cup					
1991	6-0-0	6/5	2	0	4
1995	4-1-1	6/6	2	5	9
1999	5-0-1	6/6	2	2	6
Total	15-1-2	18/17	6	7	25
Olympics					
1996	4-0-0	4/4	1	2	4
2000	3-1-1	5/5	2	2	6
Total	7-1-1	9/9	3	4	10

Source: www.soccertimes.com

Hamm (9) shows brilliant defensive effort by lunging to stop a Swedish forward from shooting the ball.

team was as good as any other. And in fact the U.S. team got off to a great start. They won their first five games by a combined score of 23-4. With just one game left to play, they were sure to finish no worse than second.

Hamm and her teammates, though, wanted to finish first. Even though they had to play the powerful Norwegians in the last game, they went all out to win. Hamm played brilliantly, especially on defense. With three minutes to go, the score was tied at one goal apiece. But the American players were getting tired fast.

Then a Norwegian player made a weak pass near her own goal. Hamm's teammate Michelle Akers beat the

In the 1993 women's college national championship game, Hamm (9) pulls the ball away from a defender, helping the Tarheels to a victory.

goalkeeper to the ball and blasted it into the net. Team USA won the game—and the first women's World Cup. Hamm's prediction had come true, and she was thrilled.

Return to UNC
After the World Cup, Hamm returned to North Carolina for two more years of college competition. The Tarheels

won the national college championship both years, and Hamm was a big reason why. Both seasons, she was voted player of the year—giving her the honor three times in all. She also won the 1994 Broderick Award given to the best college woman athlete from any sport.

Hamm did quite well off the field, too. "[I] tried to balance sports and academics as best as I could," she said. "It was not an easy task!"[4] But she studied hard, and she kept up with her classes. In 1994 she graduated with a degree in political science. She also began spending time with a student named Christiaan Corry. Soon after graduation, the two married.

With her college career over, Mia Hamm looked ahead. Her next soccer challenge would come in 1995, when she and the rest of Team USA would have to defend their World Cup title. This time the Americans would not take anybody by surprise. Every other team would be doing its best to beat them.

But Hamm was convinced that her team could win again anyway.

CHAPTER THREE

Fame and Glory

After a year of practice Team USA went to Sweden for the 1995 World Cup tournament. Women's soccer was still far from a popular sport among Americans, but more people did pay attention to the World Cup this time around. And, in particular, people began to pay attention to Mia Hamm.

In 1991 Hamm had been just one of the better players on the team. Now, after her college career, she was probably the team's biggest star. When newspapers and magazines ran stories about Team USA, they often focused on Hamm. People who read these articles learned about soccer—but they usually learned even more about Hamm.

For the first time, too, big American companies started asking the players to endorse, or advertise, their products.

Hamm was friendly, good-looking, and a star, so she was the kind of person that the companies wanted. Little by little, even people who cared nothing about soccer became familiar with the name and face of Mia Hamm.

In some ways Hamm did not like all the attention. She could not understand why people were more interested in her than in her teammates. After all, soccer was a team sport, and she was a team player. As she liked to say, "I couldn't have scored one goal without my teammates."[5]

Still, there was a good side to Hamm's growing fame. As people learned about her, they wanted to know more

Mia Hamm signs autographs for fans at a 1995 World Cup soccer match in Washington, D.C.

about women's soccer. Hamm hoped the articles and ads would help make people interested in her sport. And she was thrilled that so many children were her fans. "If I can influence young people and be a positive role model," she said once, "that's great!"[6]

Disappointment

The 1995 World Cup, though, was a big disappointment for Hamm and her teammates. After a series of early wins, they faced Norway in the fifth game. Norway was a strong team—but Team USA had defeated the Norwegians in 1991, and Hamm was sure they could do it again.

But instead, the Americans lost a very tight 1-0 game. Hamm forced herself to watch the Norwegian players celebrate their victory. "It was easily the longest ten minutes of my soccer life,"[7] she remembered afterwards. Team USA finished in third place. Hamm, though, did not give up. Instead, she wanted to get even. Next time, she vowed, her team would do better.

"Next time" came along quite soon. Olympic officials had decided to add women's soccer to the Olympic Games. The first Olympic women's tournament would be held at the 1996 Games in Atlanta, Georgia. Hamm and her teammates were determined to win the first Olympic gold medal in their sport.

The 1996 Olympics

But the 1996 Olympics started off badly. In Team USA's second game, Hamm crashed into the Swedish team's goalkeeper. She fell to the ground in pain. Her ankle was

A determined Mia Hamm sprints past three Norwegian defenders in the 1996 Olympic games.

badly sprained, and she was forced to skip the team's next game, a tie against China.

Next up was the Americans' arch-rival, Norway. If the United States won, they would play one more game, this time for the gold medal. If they lost, they could finish no higher than third. Beating the Norwegians would be hard enough, even with Hamm healthy. With her out of action the task would be much tougher.

Hamm was in great pain, but she refused to miss the game. She had the team's trainer tape her ankle as tightly as she could bear. The ankle still hurt, and she could not run well. But she played—and helped her team score its first goal, too. Team USA beat the Norwegians with a dramatic **overtime** goal. Now the United States would play China in the Olympic final.

Members of the U.S. women's soccer team pile on top of each other in celebration after clinching an overtime victory against Norway.

There had never been such excitement about a women's soccer game in the United States. Team USA, along with its star Mia Hamm, had become one of the biggest stories of the Olympics. All across the country Americans tuned their televisions to watch the match. And seventy-six thousand people saw the game in person—a new record for the sport by far.

Hamm felt better at first, and it showed. Early in the first half she made a great pass, leading to a goal. But China soon tied the game. Worse yet, Hamm's ankle had begun to throb. By the second half she was in serious pain.

But even with one bad ankle, Hamm was still more valuable on the field than on the bench. She stayed in the game. In the middle of the second half she helped her team score a second goal. That goal turned out to be the game-winner. Once again Hamm and her teammates were champions of women's soccer.

Garrett

Hamm enjoyed her team's victory, but not as much as she could have wished. Her brother Garrett, who had taught her so much about sports, had been sick for several years. He had a serious form of anemia, a disease that affects the blood. Soon after the Olympics his health got

The U.S. Olympic women's soccer team displays their gold medals for a roaring crowd of seventy-six thousand.

much worse. The only way to save his life was an operation called a bone marrow transplant, in which healthy cells from a living person are put into the patient's body.

Unfortunately, the cells could not come from just anybody. They could only come from a person whose cells closely matched Garrett's own. Usually that would be a family member. Mia would have been happy to do-

Surgeons perform a bone marrow transplant.

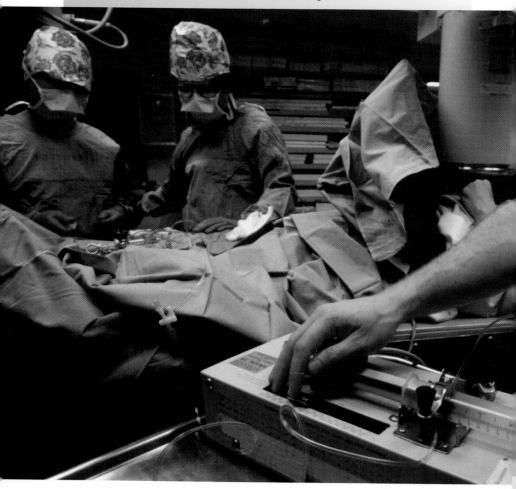

nate cells to her brother, but Garrett had been adopted. The cells from her body were not a close enough match.

Although Mia could not give cells to help her brother, she helped out in another way. In February 1997 she organized a special soccer game with some of the best players in the world. Some of the money from the ticket sales went to pay for Garrett's treatment. The rest went to scientists for research on bone marrow transplants.

That same month, doctors finally found a person whose cells would match. They quickly did the transplant. For several weeks it looked as though Garrett might recover. But being so sick for so long had made him very weak. He came down with an infection, and his body could not fight it off. That April, he died.

When Garrett died, the national team was starting a series of games across the country. Mia missed the first two games to be with her family. Then she went back to the team. "The athletic field," she said, "is where Garrett and I had so many great moments together, and I knew he would have wanted me out there."[8] Playing sports was the best way she had of honoring her brother.

World Cup 1999

The next big tournament was the 1999 World Cup, which would be played in the United States. The team looked strong in the games leading up to the tournament that summer. Hamm was playing well, too. In the spring of 1999 she scored her 109th career goal in games against other countries. That gave her more goals than any other soccer player, male or female. Not even the great men's star Pele had scored 109 goals.

Once again Hamm's team got off to a solid start in the World Cup tournament. With fans cheering from packed stadiums, Team USA won its first three games. Hamm scored twice. In the next game the team trailed a tough German team at halftime but came back to win. Next, they beat the dangerous Brazilians to qualify for the final.

The good news for the United States was that the Norwegians had lost an earlier game and were out of the tournament. The bad news was that the Chinese had qualified instead, just as they had in the Olympics. If anything, China was even stronger than in 1996. Like the Olympic final, this promised to be a great game.

The Final

This game was even more popular than the Olympic final. About 40 million Americans watched the game on TV, and ninety thousand more saw it in person. Some people paid as much as one thousand dollars for a ticket! It was difficult to believe that this was the same sport hardly anyone had cared about just eight years earlier.

The World Cup final was a great game. Team USA and China were so evenly matched that the game was tied 0-0, even after two overtime periods. But there had to be a winner, and so the game went to a **shootout**.

In a shootout, five players from each team take turns shooting **penalty kicks** against the opponent's goalkeeper. Whichever team has the most goals wins the match. The first two kickers for both teams scored. So did the third American shooter. But Team USA goalkeeper

Brandi Chastain slides to her knees, and pumps her fists after scoring the winning penalty shot in the 1999 World Cup finals.

Briana Scurry stopped the third Chinese shot. If the last two American shooters could score, the United States would win.

Hamm shot fourth for the United States. She slammed the ball past the Chinese keeper and into the net. That left it up to the last American, Brandi Chastain. She shot, the keeper lunged, and the ball went into the goal. The fans went wild.

So did Team USA. Mia Hamm and the Americans owned the World Cup once more.

Moving On

Winning the Olympics and the World Cup gave women's soccer a huge boost. All of a sudden it seemed that everyone knew about the players on the national team. For the first time, Mia Hamm was not the only well-known player on Team USA.

Still, Hamm remained by far the most famous. Now she was truly a celebrity. Crowds of people asked her for her autograph. She appeared in ads for shoes, sport drinks, energy bars, a soccer-playing doll, and even a bank. Fans bought Team USA jerseys with her name and number on the back. *People* magazine even chose her as one of the country's "50 Most Beautiful People."

Once again Hamm was a little bit embarrassed by the attention. "I'm no better than a lot of people on this

Mia Hamm holds her new soccer cleat in an ad for her sponsor, Nike.

U.S. team,"[9] she told a reporter during the World Cup tournament. Kristine Lilly was a much better passer than she was, said Hamm, and Michelle Akers had a harder shot. Besides, she repeated, soccer was a team effort.

But Hamm could not escape the attention no matter how much she tried. She was more comfortable with it now than she had been before. She had seen how her own fame had helped make women's soccer a sport that people cared about. And she knew that her teammates did not really mind the extra attention she received.

Other Activities

Hamm also used her celebrity to help others. She had always appeared at soccer clinics for young players, and she kept doing it long after she became a star. She spent a lot of time teaching children and teenagers how to improve their skills, and she enjoyed it very much.

Hamm stayed active in fighting the disease that killed her brother, too. She organized another "Garrett Game" to raise more money for research into bone marrow transplants. Later, she started an organization, the Mia Hamm Foundation, which also gave more money for research as well as for encouraging girls and women to play sports.

Finally, Hamm also did her best to take time for herself. Soon after their marriage, her husband had become

Nancy Lieberman-Cline (left), Mia Hamm (middle), and Juli Inkster (right) pose for the Women's Sports Foundation, an organization that promotes women athletes.

a pilot in the marines. Between his flying and her soccer, the two of them were often apart. When she had a day off Hamm liked to spend time with him.

Hamm also enjoyed playing golf, reading, and movies, either on her own or with her teammates. Sometimes she and her friends from the team played card games in which the losers had to give cookies to the winner. These interests took her away from sports, but Hamm knew that relaxing was important, too. As she told her young fans, "You can't stay focused on soccer all the time."[10]

More Soccer

Hamm still continued to devote most of her time to soccer. Though many people called her the best player in the world, Hamm herself was not so sure. There were parts of her game that she thought she could improve. Great as she was, she kept working to make herself even better.

Since the 1999 World Cup, though, Hamm has had some disappointments in soccer. She played in the 2000 Olympics with Team USA, but the team lost the final to Norway in a thrilling overtime game. "We left everything out there on the field, and you can't do anything more,"[11] sighed Hamm after the match.

Another disappointment came in 2001. For years Hamm had wished for an American women's soccer league, and in 2001 she got her wish. The new league was called the Women's United Soccer Association, or WUSA for short. Hamm hoped that the league would

Mia Hamm (left) and Julie Foudy, founding players of the WUSA professional women's soccer league, pose for a photo before the first season.

keep Americans thinking about her sport when there were no Olympics or World Cup tournaments.

Hamm played for the Washington Freedom, one of the league's eight teams. But the team did not play well. The Freedom finished seventh with a record of six wins, twelve losses, and three ties. For Hamm, who was used to winning, it was hard to be on the losing end of the game so often.

Mia Hamm of the Washington Freedom stands with a dejected look on her face, waiting for the final seconds of the game to tick away.

And Hamm did not have a good season herself. She had hurt her left knee just before the 2001 season began. The leg did not heal very well, and she could not play the way she wanted to. Opposing players guarded her so closely, too, that she had trouble passing and shooting. She finished the year with just six goals in twenty-one games.

Unfortunately, the knee injury just would not go away. In early 2002 she had surgery on her leg and had to begin that season on the injured list. Sitting on the bench was hard for Hamm. She cheered for her team and gave advice to other players when she could—but it was not the same as playing.

The Future

Mia Hamm continues to work on being the best soccer player she can be. When she is healthy, she practices as often as possible. Now that her thirtieth birthday is past, she knows she has to work even harder. Many athletes are at their best when they are in their twenties. Once they get older, they begin to slow down.

Still, Hamm has always been a very hard worker who keeps herself in great shape. There is no reason to think she will lose her skills quickly, so she expects to keep playing for at least a few more years. She would love to help defend the World Cup title in 2003, and she would like another Olympic gold medal before she retires.

Some people think Hamm might want to coach after her playing career is over. Others say she could become an announcer for soccer games on TV. Or Hamm might decide to leave the sport altogether.

But that will be later. Until that time comes she will stay on the field and do what she does best: play soccer.

Notes

Chapter One: Becoming an Athlete
1. Mia Hamm, *Go for the Goal! A Champion's Guide to Winning in Soccer and Life*. New York: HarperCollins, 1999, p. 12.
2. Hamm, *Go for the Goal!*, p. 29.

Chapter Two: Titles and Championships
3. Hamm, *Go for the Goal!*, p. 30.
4. Quoted in Gregg Mazzola, "Goals," *Coach and Athletic Director*, December 1998, p. 44+.

Chapter Three: Fame and Glory
5. Hamm, *Go for the Goal!*, p. 9.
6. Quoted in Mazzola, "Goals," p. 44+.
7. Hamm, *Go for the Goal!*, p. 197.
8. Hamm, *Go for the Goal!*, p. 39.

Chapter Four: Moving On
9. Quoted in *Current Biography Yearbook 1999*, p. 246.
10. Hamm, *Go for the Goal!*, p. 199.
11. Quoted in CBS *Sportsline*, "U.S. Women Upset over Loss but Maintain Their Unity," Associated Press. http://cbs.sportsline.com.

Glossary

developmental team: A team of players who are less concerned with winning games and more concerned with improving their skills.

forward: The position most in charge of shooting and scoring. Forwards play nearest the other team's goal.

goalkeeper: The player most responsible for keeping the ball out of the net. Goalkeepers are the only players allowed to use their hands.

Olympics: An international event held every four years, at which many sports are played. Winners are given medals.

overtime: An extra fifteen-minute period played if the game is tied after regulation.

penalty kick: A kick taken by one team when the other team cannot interfere. A team gets a penalty kick when an opponent commits a foul, such as by touching the ball with a hand or knocking down another player.

shootout: A way of deciding a soccer game when it is tied after two overtime periods. Five shooters from each side take turns trying to score against only the opposing goalkeeper.

World Cup: An international soccer tournament held every four years. Women's tournaments began in 1991.

For Further Exploration

Matt Christopher, *On the Field with Mia Hamm*. Boston: Little, Brown, 1998. Detailed description of Hamm's life and career; for young adults. Despite the copyright date, the book includes information on the 1999 World Cup.

Wayne R. Coffey, *Meet the Women of American Soccer: An Inside Look at America's Team*. New York: Scholastic, 1999. A well-illustrated book focusing on the members of Team USA. Includes information about Hamm as well as her teammates.

David Fisher, *Mia Hamm*. Andrews McMeel, 2000. Biographical information, focusing on the 1999 World Cup.

Rachel Rutledge, *Mia Hamm: Striking Superstar*. Brookfield, CT: Millbrook, 2000. A biographical account running through the end of World Cup 1999. Includes sidebars and quotes by and about Hamm.

Robert Schnakenberg, *Mia Hamm*. Philadelphia: Chelsea House, 2001. A well-illustrated biography covering Hamm's life to just before the 1999 World Cup.

John Albert Torres, *Mia Hamm*. Mitchell Lane, 1999. A short biography, including information on Hamm's personal life as well as her soccer career.

Index

Picture Credits

Cover photo: © Duomo/CORBIS
Allsport, USA, 20, 23, 25
Associated Press, AP, 10, 26, 27, 35, 37
Associated Press, The Chapel Hill News, 16
Associated Press, The San Francisco Examiner, 31
Shaun Botterill/Allsport, 19
© Duomo/CORBIS, 5, 14
Brandy Noon, 18
Tony Quinn/Allsport, 38
© Reuters NewMedia, Inc./CORBIS, 34
© Ted Spiegel/CORBIS, 28
Rick Stewart/Allsport, 11
Scott Weersing/Allsport, 8
YearbookArchives.com, 7

About the Author

Stephen Currie is the author of more than forty books, including *The Salem Witch Trials* in KidHaven's World History series. He has also written other books about sports and athletes. He lives in New York state with his family; his daughter, Irene, plays youth soccer and helped with the research for this book.